My Best Book of
Extinct Animals

Christiane Gunzi

KINGFISHER

KINGFISHER

Kingfisher Publications Plc
New Penderel House
283–288 High Holborn
London WC1V 7HZ

www.kingfisherpub.com

Created for Kingfisher Publications Plc
by Picthall & Gunzi Limited

Author and editor: Christiane Gunzi
Designer: Dominic Zwemmer
Consultant: Barbara Taylor-Cork

Illustrators: Michael Langham-Rowe,
Angus McBride, Richard Hook, Peter
Goodfellow, Ray Grinaway, Bernard
Long, Tony Morris, Nicki Palin

First published by Kingfisher
Publications Plc 2004

10 9 8 7 6 5 4 3 2 1

1TR/0304/WKT/MAR(MAR)/128KMA
1TS/0804/WKT/MAR(MAR)/128MA/F

A CIP catalogue record for this book
is available from the British Library.

ISBN 0 7534 0959 3

Printed in China

Contents

4 What is extinction?

6 Extinct animals of the world

14 The end of the Ice Age

16 Where did the dodo go?

24 The great survivors

26 Extinction and us

8 How we know

10 When the dinosaurs died

12 Amazing reptiles

18 The biggest birds ever

20 The quagga's tale

22 Extinction in Australia

28 Wildlife at risk

30 A future for us all

31 Glossary
32 Index

What is extinction?

Extinction is the end of a species or a group of animals or plants. Extinct animals are those that no longer exist, such as dinosaurs and woolly mammoths. Before humans existed, extinctions were caused by natural events and they took many years. But since humans arrived, many animal species have died out in a very short space of time.

A change of climate

Many animals, such as mammoths, died out at the end of the last Ice Age, when the climate became warmer.

Destroying habitats

People are damaging the habitats where wild animals live. Huge areas of forest have been cut down to make space for farms and buildings. This is the biggest cause of extinction today.

Fishing too much

At the moment we are catching far too many fish in the oceans. This is known as 'over-harvesting'. If we do not stop over-fishing very soon many species of fish will become extinct.

Introducing species

When people first travelled to other countries, they took dogs, cats and pigs with them. These animals competed with the animals that already lived there, and ate their eggs and young.

Mass extinctions

Major extinctions are known as 'mass extinctions'. In a mass extinction many species die out at one time. There have been at least five big mass extinctions. Many scientists believe that the last one was caused when an enormous meteor crashed into Earth. It would have caused dramatic changes in climate, including floods.

A huge meteor probably brought about the end of dinosaurs and pterosaurs.

Extinct animals of the world

Over billions of years of life on earth, millions of species of animals have evolved and then died out.

The most well-known extinct animals are the dinosaurs, which died out 65 million years ago. But many animals have become extinct since then, and others will continue to die out in the future. The Tasmanian wolf, or thylacine, became extinct only 100 years ago.

Pteranodon died out 65 million years ago.

Archelon died out 65 million years ago.

Argentinosaurus died out 65 million years ago.

Dunkleosteus (left) died out 360 million years ago.

The early extinctions

The mass extinction of dinosaurs and other animals was a huge event, but there were at least four other mass extinctions before that one. Dunkleosteus and lots of other sea creatures became extinct 360 million years ago, in the Devonian period.

Mosasaurs died out 65 million years ago.

Ammonites died out 65 million years ago.

Platybelodon
died out 1.75 million years ago.

Steller's sea cow
died out in 1768.

Giant moa died
out at the end
of the 1600s.

Macrauchenias
died out 20,000
years ago.

Dodo died out
in 1681.

Quagga died out
in 1870.

Smilodon
died out 10,000 years ago.

Carolina parakeet
died out in 1920.

Woolly rhinoceros died
out 10,000 years ago.

Thylacine (Tasmanian wolf)
died out in the 1930s.

How we know

Scientists find out about extinct animals by studying fossils. The fossilized bones of dinosaurs show us what these amazing reptiles looked like, and how they lived millions of years ago. The fossilized shells that you find on beaches belong to sea creatures that swam in the oceans even before the dinosaurs existed!

Oceans of animals

About 600 million years ago, a huge variety of wildlife lived in the oceans, and sea creatures with shells began to appear. But these died out in a series of mass extinctions, possibly due to changes in sea levels. Their fossils still remain today!

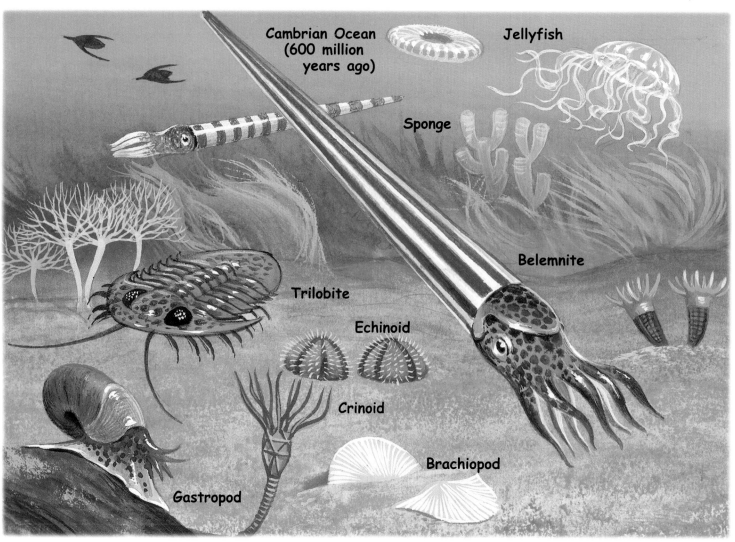

Cambrian Ocean (600 million years ago)

Jellyfish

Sponge

Belemnite

Trilobite

Echinoid

Crinoid

Brachiopod

Gastropod

How an ammonite fossil is formed

1 When a shelled sea creature dies, its shell falls on to the seabed. The animal's soft body dissolves but the shell remains.

2 As the sea gently washes over the shell, sand and sediment gradually fill up the inside. Eventually the shell is totally covered.

3 Over millions of years, the sand and sediment harden into rock in the shape of the shelled creature. A fossil has formed.

4 After many more years, a fossil hunter can break open a rock to discover the fossil of an extinct ammonite hidden inside!

Finding fossils

Studying fossils helps us to understand more about animals. There are fossils of ammonites on many beaches of the world. It is very exciting to look at the remains of an animal that lived in the ocean 200 million years ago!

These children are looking at an ammonite fossil with their teacher.

When the dinosaurs died

For 165 million years, dinosaurs ruled the earth. Then, 65 million years ago, at the end of the Cretaceous period, they all died out. This is the most famous mass extinction, even though it was not as big as some of the earlier ones. When the dinosaurs became extinct, many other animals did too. Amazingly, some survived, including insects, lizards, crocodiles, a few mammals, birds and many fish and other sea creatures.

Dinosaurs could not survive when huge dust clouds blocked out the warm sun for many years.

10

Dangerous dust cloud

The end of the dinosaurs was probably due to the climate becoming cooler. At this time there were massive volcanoes pumping ash into the sky, and a huge meteor crashed into the Earth. Ash and dust made the planet dark and cold for years.

Amazing reptiles

Many amazing reptiles died out when the dinosaurs did. These included enormous flying reptiles and huge, powerful sea reptiles. Some swimming reptiles, such as liopleurodon, were as long as the biggest long-necked dinosaurs. By the end of the Cretaceous period, pterosaurs, mosasaurs and plesiosaurs were all extinct. From this time onwards, mammals began to rule the earth.

Mega crocodile

The largest crocodile that ever lived was deinosuchus. It was 15m long and may have weighed two tonnes. This huge reptile ate dinosaurs!

Reptiles of the sea

Sea reptiles such as platecarpus and liopleurodon were fierce predators. Some sea reptiles grew to gigantic sizes, and were as big as sperm whales today. Their teeth were twice the size of T-Rex's teeth!

Platecarpus was a mosasaur about 7m long.

Elasmosaurus' neck was over half the length of its body.

Ammonites swam using jet propulsion.

Reptiles of the sky

The biggest flying creatures ever were reptiles called pterosaurs. Pterosaurs had wings like a bat's, and their bodies were probably furry.

Quetzalcoatlus was the biggest pterosaur, with a 10m wingspan.

Pteranodons were pterosaurs that ate fish, crabs and insects.

Liopleurodon was a plesiosaur over 10m long.

Archelon was a big sea turtle about the size of a small car.

Tylosaurus was a large carnivorous mosasaur up to 12m long.

The Irish elk was a deer about the size of a moose, and it had the biggest antlers ever known.

Woolly rhinoceroses grazed on grasslands and tundra.

Woolly mammoths fiercely protected their young from attackers, such as lions.

Mighty mammoths

With their long, hairy coats, woolly mammoths were well adapted to life in the last Ice Age. In summer, they probably moulted, like musk oxen. Most woolly mammoths were the size of today's elephants, but they had massive tusks for defence against enemies.

14

The end of the Ice Age

About 10,000 years ago, at the end of the last Ice Age, many mammals died out. Summer and winter temperatures became so extreme that big plant eaters such as woolly mammoths, woolly rhinos and cave bears could not adapt to the changes in climate. They were also hunted by humans for their meat and fur, and by the end of the Ice Age they were extinct.

Cave bears lived in caves close to forests, and were the size of the biggest grizzly bears today.

Cave lions hunted plant eaters such as deer and became extinct when their prey did.

Discovering the past

In 1977, a bulldozer driver in Siberia discovered the frozen carcass of a whole baby mammoth. It was the same size as a baby elephant, only its ears were smaller. Using special radiocarbon dating, scientists discovered that the mammoth had died 40,000 years ago. It still had some hair on its legs!

Where did the dodo go?

The dodo is probably the best-known extinct animal of all. This large, heavy bird was discovered on the island of Mauritius, in the Indian Ocean, in the 1500s. But, 170 years later, there were no dodos left. Dodos had no real enemies on their island home until European sailors arrived, so they were not afraid of people. Dodos could not fly, and were so slow-moving that they were easy to catch. The sailors killed them mainly for food.

Introducing new species

When sailors travelled to other islands they took domestic animals with them. They introduced dogs, cats, pigs and also rats to islands where these animals had never lived before. These 'introduced species' competed with the native animals for their food and territory.

Portuguese sailors travelled to the island of Mauritius, taking domestic animals with them.

Disturbed by dogs

The dogs, pigs and other animals that the sailors brought to the island of Mauritius disturbed the dodos on their nests. These animals may also have eaten the birds' eggs.

All a dodo had for protection against attackers was its big, strong beak.

The biggest birds ever

About 400 hundred years ago, there were giant moas in New Zealand and elephant birds in Madagascar. These birds could not fly and were probably related to ostriches. Moas did not even have wings! Some moas were the size of a turkey, but others were almost 2m tall. They lived in forests and fed on plants. People hunted giant moas until they were extinct by the end of the 1600s. Elephant birds died out at about the same time.

Enormous eggs

Elephant birds were about 3m tall, and their eggs were the size of basketballs! These African birds may have died out because people kept stealing their huge eggs for food.

Egg   Basketball

Terrifying talons

A moa's only enemy, apart from humans, was the huge Haast eagle. This was the biggest, most powerful eagle ever known. The Haast eagle had talons as big as a tiger's claws, and it could swoop down at 80km/h to grab a moa. Haast eagles died out when their moa prey became extinct.

Haast eagles
attacked giant
moas in their
forest habitat.

The quagga's tale

About 120 years ago, huge herds of animals called quaggas ran free on the African plains. They were killed for their meat and skin, and now they do not exist. Recently, scientists have discovered that the quagga was actually a type of zebra. Now, scientists are trying to breed zebras with markings similar to the quagga. Maybe quaggas will return to Africa one day.

The last quagga

Wild quaggas died out in about 1878. In 1883, the last quagga died at Amsterdam zoo, in Holland. She had lived there for 16 years.

Hunting the whole herd

In the 1830s, Dutch farmers called Boers, who lived in southern Africa, hunted herds of quagga on horseback. They shot many thousands of them with guns, mainly for food.

Quaggas looked like zebras, but they had fewer stripes.

A strange sight

During the 1830s, quaggas were transported to Europe from Africa. These unusual animals were so easy to tame that they were used to pull carriages. Nobody realised then that less than 50 years later quaggas would be extinct.

Extinction in Australia

There are many fascinating animals in Australia, but there used to be even more. Once there were 20 different kinds of giant kangaroo, and wolves and lions with pouches! In the past 200 years, half of all the native mammals of Australia have become extinct. This is due mainly to hunting and habitat destruction. Other large animals, such as giant lizards, have also died out.

Kangaroo carnivores

One extinct kangaroo was a meat-eater. Ekaltadeta was the size of a large dog. It had long teeth for biting prey and probably used its front legs to hold its food!

Biggest ever

Mammals with pouches, called marsupials, first appeared in the middle of the Cretaceous period. Procoptodon was the biggest kangaroo, and the marsupial lion was the largest carnivorous Australian mammal. Diprotodon was the biggest marsupial ever! All of these are now extinct. Giant reptiles are extinct too.

Procoptodon was 3m tall, with long arms.

Diprotodon was about the size of a cow.

The marsupial lion was 1.5m from head to tail.

Giant echidna was 1m long and weighed 30kg.

Quinkana was a 7m crocodile with long legs.

The giant ripper lizard was called 'megalania'.

22

The wolf with a pouch

The thylacine, or Tasmanian wolf, once lived all over Australia and Tasmania. But when European settlers arrived they began to kill them. Thylacines ate birds, kangaroos and small rodents. They also preyed on sheep, so farmers often shot, trapped and poisoned them. The last known thylacine died in a zoo in 1936.

Thylacines could open their mouths extremely wide to bite large animals.

The great survivors

Scientists are not sure why some species survive better than others. Animals such as sharks, crocodiles and insects are so well-suited to their environments that they have survived unchanged for millions of years. The best survivors are usually animals that can move fast, breed quickly and eat a variety of foods. Insects do all of these things, and they are able to live in a wide range of places because they are so small. This makes them great survivors.

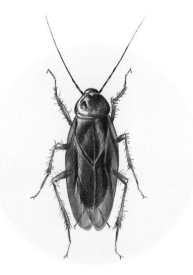

Incredible insect

Cockroaches have existed for 300 million years, and there are about 4,000 kinds. These insects can survive for three months without food and a month without water.

Amazing reptile

There have been crocodiles on earth for 200 million years, and they have hardly changed since the time of the dinosaurs. Crocodiles have the most advanced brains of all reptiles. They have an extra eyelid to protect their eyes, and they can close their nostrils, ears and throat to dive underwater.

King of the ocean

Sharks are fish that live in every ocean of the world. They have survived for more than 350 million years. One of the earliest kinds of shark was about 12m long. Each of its massive teeth was about as big as a child's hand!

Not extinct yet

In 1938, an extraordinary fish called a coelacanth was found living in the Indian Ocean. Up until then, scientists believed that this type of fish had been extinct for about 70 million years. The ancient fish has been nicknamed a 'living fossil'.

With its armour-plating, powerful tail and sharp teeth, the Nile crocodile is a perfect predator.

Extinction and us

According to many scientists a sixth mass extinction is happening right now. They think that humans are the cause. As we pollute the rivers and seas with toxic chemicals, and cut down and burn the forests, we are destroying the homes of many species. Animals are dying out at an incredible rate, including unusual insects and sea creatures. It may take millions of years for these animal species to be replaced by new ones.

A fragile world

When people swim over reefs and touch the corals, they damage this delicate habitat and can kill the corals. Reefs that are close to the coast are also damaged by mining, as they become buried under layers of mud.

The anchors of boats cause a lot of damage to corals on the reef.

Over-fishing in the oceans

One of the most serious problems for the environment today is over-harvesting of the oceans. Fish are being caught and killed much faster than they can lay eggs. The luxury seafood known as caviar is actually fish eggs, which come from the sturgeon. Surprisingly, some of the most endangered fish of all (see pictures below) are cod and tuna.

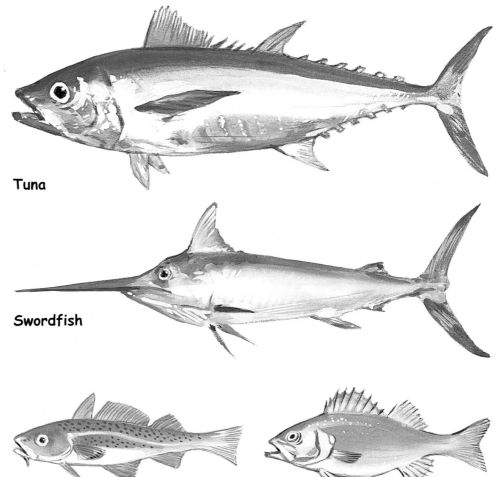

Tuna

Swordfish

Cod

Sea bass

Sturgeon

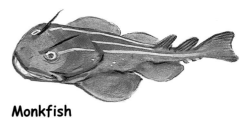

Monkfish

The riches of the rainforest

The Amazon rainforest, in South America, is the richest wildlife habitat on earth. It is the home of billions of creatures. All of them are in danger of extinction because so much of the rainforest has been damaged by people.

Spider monkey

Macaws

Harpy eagle

Toucan

Boa constrictor

Jaguar

Capuchin monkey

Amazon parrot

Hummingbird

Blue morpho butterfly

Poison-dart frog

Katydid

Wildlife at risk

The forests are the world's most important habitats. Rainforests, in particular, are home to a huge variety of insects, birds, mammals, reptiles and amphibians. So far, zoologists have been able to identify and name only a small number of the billions of different creatures on earth. But there are millions more still to discover, especially insects and other tiny creatures. Sadly, some of these animals may become extinct even before we have time to identify them.

Orang-utans in danger

All the great apes, such as orang-utans and gorillas are in danger, due to the destruction of the rainforests. Within ten to 20 years, orang-utans will probably be extinct in the wild.

People and trees

In Asia and South America, some local people earn a living by cutting down trees. They sell the wood to other, richer countries for making furniture. Wildlife organizations are trying to stop this trade in exotic wood because these trees are very rare and the rainforests are disappearing.

These trees will be made into furniture.

A future for us all

Humans are the most powerful and successful species on earth. We are likely to survive for a long time. To make sure that tigers, whales and other endangered animals survive too, we must take more care of their habitats, such as rainforests, oceans and polar regions. If we do not act in a responsible way, some of the most magnificent animals that ever lived may become extinct in our lifetimes.

Tamarins in a zoo

Saving the tamarins

Golden lion tamarins live in zoos because their rainforest home in Brazil has been cut down. They are kept behind glass to protect them from human diseases. Some of these monkeys have now been returned to the wild.

Too late for the tiger?

There are now only a few thousand wild tigers left. Wildlife organizations are trying to protect these cats, but sadly it may be too late.

Bengal tigers are in danger because people are mining in their territory.

Glossary

adapt To be able to change to fit in with new surroundings. Some animals and plants are good at adapting to change.

amphibian Certain animals, such as frogs and toads, which first appeared on earth during the Devonian period.

camouflage The different colours and markings on an animal that help it to hide in the wild.

carcass The dead body of an animal, often one that is killed for food.

carnivore An animal, such as a shark, hawk or tiger, that eats meat.

climate The conditions of an area, such as its weather and temperature.

Cretaceous period A time period in earth's history which lasted for 65 million years, in which flowering plants first appeared.

Devonian period A time period which lasted for 50 million years, in which amphibians first appeared.

domestic animal An animal, such as a dog, that lives with, or is kept by, people.

endangered Animals, such as the Bengal tiger, that are now in danger of becoming extinct.

evolve To develop over time. It can take millions of years for a new species to evolve.

extinct An animal or plant that has died out forever.

fossil The remains of a plant or animal that died millions of years ago, preserved in rock.

habitat An animal's habitat is its natural home.

Ice Age The period during which most of earth's surface was covered in ice.

introduced species Animals that have been taken to a country where they did not ever live before.

mammals Animals, such as bears, which have fur or hair, give birth to live young, and feed them milk.

meteor A rock-like object from outer space that enters the Earth's atmosphere.

native Animals or plants that live in a specific place. The dodo was native to Mauritius.

predators Animals that hunt and prey on other animals.

prey Animals that are hunted and eaten by carnivores.

radiocarbon dating A scientific test carried out on rocks, fossils and trees to find out their age.

reptiles Certain cold-blooded animals with scaly skin, such as lizards.

species A group of animals that look alike and are closely related to each other.

territory An area of land where an animal lives and which it defends against other animals.

Index

A
Amazon rainforest 28, 29
ammonites 6, 9, 12
archelon 6, 13
argentinosaurus 6
Australian animals 22–23

B
Bengal tigers 30

C
Carolina parakeets 7
cave bears 15
climate 4, 5, 11, 15
cockroaches 24
cod 27
coelacanths 25
Cretaceous period 10, 12, 22
crocodiles 10, 12, 24

D
deinosuchus 12
Devonian period 6
dinosaurs 4, 5, 6, 8, 10-11, 12, 24
diprotodon 22
dodos 7, 16–17
dunkleosteus 6

E
ekaltadeta 22
elephant birds 18
endangered animals 30
extinction 4–5, 22, 26, 28

F
fossils 8–9, 25

G
giant echidnas 22
golden lion tamarins 30
gorillas 29

H
Haast eagles 18, 19

I
Ice Age 4, 14–15
insects 10, 24, 26, 29
Irish elk 14

K
kangaroos 22, 23

L
lions 15, 22
liopleurodon 12, 13

M
macrauchenias 7
mammals 10, 12, 22, 29
marsupials 22
mass extinctions 5, 8, 10, 26
megalania 22
meteor 5, 11
moas 7, 18, 19
mosasaurs 6, 12, 13

N
Nile crocodiles 25

O
orang-utans 29
over-harvesting 4, 27

P
platecarpus 12
platybelodon 7
plesiosaurs 12, 13
pollution 26
procoptodon 22
pteranodon 6, 13
pterosaurs 5, 12, 13

Q
quaggas 7, 20–21
quetzalcoatlus 13
quinkana 22

R
radiocarbon dating 15
reptiles 8, 12–13, 22, 24, 29

S
sharks 24, 25
smilodon 7
Steller's sea cow 7

T
Tasmanian wolf 6, 7, 23
thylacine see Tasmanian wolf
tuna 27
tylosaurus 13

W
wildlife organizations 29, 30
woolly mammoths 4, 14, 15
woolly rhinoceroses 7, 14, 15

Z
zebras 20
zoologists 29